Pam and Hap

by Nathan Howell
illustrated by Mark Corcoran

Practice Decodable 13

McGraw Hill Education

Bothell, WA • Chicago, IL • Columbus, OH • New York, NY

MHEonline.com

Send all inquiries to:
McGraw-Hill Education
8787 Orion Place
Columbus, OH 43240

ISBN: 978-0-02-146276-6
MHID: 0-02-146276-3

Printed in China.

8 9 10 11 12 DSS 27 26 25 24 23

Hap is in a hat.

A hat is on Pam.

Pam pats a hat.

Pam taps a hat.

Is Hap in a hat?

Hap sat on Pam!